SALTED ROOK

SALTED ROOK

DOUGLAS PAYNE

Chest-O-Drawers Press

Acknowledgments

The author would like to thank Sydney Brown especially, along with Ilya Kaminsky, Sherwin Bitsui, and Karl Sherlock for their feedback and suggestions on several of these poems during the writing and editing process.

Additional thanks for their help and support during this book's creation are owed to Cass Lynch, Norman Dubie, Dennis Cooper, Felicia Williams, Ron Salisbury, Marisol Benter, Steve Bedle, and Jack Geist.

The sonnet cycle "Crown of Thorns" was inspired by Malachi Blacks's "Quarantine."
"Loneliness as a Paper Bag" first appeared in *San Diego Writers, Ink A Year in Ink*, Vol. 5.

Salted Rook
Copyright © 2017 by Douglas Payne
All rights reserved
First edition
Chest-O-Drawers Press (A Literary Project of Grossmont College)
El Cajon, California
http://www.grossmont.edu/english/cw

Cover Design: Karl Sherlock
Interior Layout: Adam Deutsch

ISBN-10: 0-943899-04-5
ISBN-13: 978-1-943899-04-3

Printed in the United States

Table of Contents

Townes Van Zandt at the Aero Club 1
Sketches of Spain 3
My Grandfather's Heart Was a Prison Bed 4
Dream-Sick 5
Loneliness as a Paper Bag 7
Elegy for Thomas 8
Stomped 10
The Burningly Majestic Syllabus That Terrified Your Parents 11
Let No Light Enter 13
Love Like Glass Enamel 15
Hands 17
Dream of the Staircase 18
Crown of Thorns
    Dawn 19
    Mourning 20
    Meridian 21
    Dusk 22
    Nocturne 23
    Twilight 24
Little Girl Blue 25
Shasta Becomes a Bird 26
A Hymn to Your Hip 27
Camera Lucida 28
Down in the Ditch 29
Soft Violet 30
Excrement 31
Driftwood 32
You Will Be Gray 34

For my grandfather,
who pointed me to Magister Ludi.

For my grandmother—
there are flowers here

Townes Van Zandt at the Aero Club

The farthest corner of the bar
is the only place to hide
from the whorish sun that spreads
to brighten the black back wall
when the door opens.

A man brands the floor with his footprints
thick with screams of trampled foxgloves.
I stare at his shadow, a worn desert highway,
my pilsner glass shaking in my grip
as I attempt to create new words

for the condition of his skin—
the colors of a knapsack, the contours of sand dunes.

He is a phantasm of dusted taverns—
a dead flower print shirt, a secondhand suit.
He stands long like a back porch evening song,
but makes no sound, not one.

He sits on a stool, back a curved turtle shell,
a century-old shotgun barrel bent with weather.
A lake-deep bellow stumbles through his lips
when he asks the bartender for a shot of Old Crow.

He turns to me and says,
"What you're drinking smells like my engine,
takes me back to when I sniffed airplane glue."

He talks through half a bottle
about the blues, how it rides
across your back like a little sister
and rots there for years,
sprouting flowers that smell
of bone dust and stolen tires.

He tells me he traded
his days for a melody, a loved
girl for every chord
and he would not talk about
the lyrics or what drove him
to put down the words.

He stifles a sigh, lines up another round,
says that his soul fell off a truck somewhere
back in Austin, after the shocks of lightning
lined his eyes with visions of the clock,
the hands running forward.

He tells me this is a stolen moment
and all time is the cost for a song.
We will live beneath night's veil,
alone with the gleam of the broken
guitar string, and the reflecting light
in the last red drop of wine.

Sketches of Spain

1
The first pressing
from 1960 loved
by white dust,
ridges of gold
liquor, grandfather
beat his wife inside
its bayonet of sound.

2
The bloody moon,
crusted back pressed
to the battered wall of night,
hovering over the crumbled
bladder, the crushed cape
of the matador.

3
The day dawns.
A pressed blue suit
plays a melting trumpet
for a sunrise funeral.

Daylight hooked on the horse,
nods off against the dreams
of his children, dead arm weighing
down their throats, erasing
Come back, erasing
Is he breathing?

4
Through tears, the moon multiplies:
a thousand mourners singing psalms,
a dusty procession dispersed by wasps.
The moon is a smiling lady to strangers,
a pile of broken teeth.

My Grandfather's Heart Was a Prison Bed

left to burn in a field of bruised corn,
his eyes scorched geese
searching for a lake of ether.

Arms cracked pool cues in the mud,
and hands a black bible
halved by a switchblade.

His knees were greased
in the beaten concrete, his voice
a sleeping electric chair,
his tongue a table saw wailing
at the mouth of a barn.

My grandfather's teeth
were tea leaves and almonds,
his skull an oak steeped
in gray paint and wool,
his back an oil well
screaming.

His coffin an empty domino
case, its contents collapsing
coal dark on the table.

Dream-Sick

Confession is drab linoleum
when the world
is perched on a rocking horse.

My loose throat throws rivers
to a ghost-white bowl, my halo
burning holes in the bathroom door.

I chew the chicken bones of boyhood.

My wooden legs make way
to sunken sofa sleep.
Dream-sick,

bulging from my brain
the yesterdays cling
like liver-aches.

Bright shine
mutes emptiness—
to forget a night again

without a body to claw,
without breath in my ear,
courted by silent curses.

My eyes pin harsh hymns
to the ceiling, my lips
spit cold threats at the walls.

I will burn up the churchyards,
break the bells that ring sweet
when at last my legs stop trembling.

I will catch
an angel in this empty bottle
and she will sing through the dark.

Loneliness as a Paper Bag

A dry turkey sandwich
or the head of a Greek god
sawed off the stone body—
to pull it out and just chew
on the thoughts.

Perhaps a raw pint:
jazz cooking cold winter air,
notes of smoke and honey—
those springtime girls running past,
their taste of sweet grass.

Crumpled rejoinders
that most toss away:
Marx mincing Hegel,
or god as a bum
in old dancing shoes,

bringing it all back homeless.

Elegy for Thomas

Broke into homes in the warm spring thaw
groping cold doorknobs, copped petty cash, drunken palms
grasped the bluebird weight of a small thong snatched from a
drawer.

The oak table, ivory blinds and noon-bright corners:
Each worth more than crafting candles,
cooking dope in Houston

or picking tomatoes in the fields
of California, the skin peeled
from sun-washed hands like flags of surrender.

They will send you back to Chino for this:
making a pot of coffee in this unknown kitchen,
the bubbling drip drumming into the glass

as the wife turns the deadbolt,
the husband locks the car,
the daughter bounds upstairs in tears.

You had a daughter once
you remember, as you plummet
through the back door into the alley.

In your dream, the flood of air
from her small lungs blowing
out trick candles on a birthday cake,

not blood or the ditch
they found her cradled in at twenty-eight,
the rain darkened news print tattooed with her name.

You crash and fold beneath the trash cans, shattered back
cooled on brick, lips dried to bleeding, you grin out black

and gray teeth, like the keys of a landfill piano on fire.

They will send you back to Chino for this, but so what?

You can only hold on so long to this April day,
this little house and its picked lock slips out
from your drunken hands, your fingers

clutching piss damp bedsheets now
in this worn-down room, the bubbling drip
turns through the tube into a tiny blue vein.

You are stretching through the white glow
of your bones, straight up like a spade
in droughted dirt,

you're screaming through
the weightless zero of your mouth
some cloaked admission of another crime, another loss.

You can't own this.
Too much.
Too long.

Stomped

The blue beat is a blade punched through
the tarpaulin of dusk, or a mermaid sliced
like sushi and dropped into the drooling mouth
of mother ocean. The blue beat of their boots

against the splintered crooks of skull
is a maritime feeling, this oily taste
of weeping on his teeth as his jaw
throws a flat note against a rusted steel

trash basket or an aluminum ball bat
that hollers and howls like the men,
the blue beat of their boots
against his dreaming head:

watching orange clouds of brushfire
beside an empty theater showing forever
the death throes of his Fourth Grade crush,
or fumbled kiss of lips that taste

of cinnamon and sawdust spilling
out onto his clothes, spilling out
onto the floor a jagged piece of bone
and lumpy strings and bits of veins
against the blue beat of their boots.

The Burningly Majestic Syllabus That Terrified Your Parents

Description: This course involves a careful examination of sad people sitting at desks, crying. Emphases are on poetic process ("schizophrenia," the impossible penetration of that fuckless androgyne known as meaning, and the hermeneutical erasure of insanity in the magician's mind. No belt-cracking daddies. No pill-chewing mommies anymore. We will learn how the magician hears a song in his palms as he grips wood and bumps keys, and how the rest of humanity is caught on mute.

Organization: This is a lecture course and I will serve as Mussolini. However, this course encourages collaborative dialogue, and then I will be your maharishi, baby. Every other class, there will be a small oral exercise where no one speaks and everyone starts to itch. People will look for found poetry in the frosted lights, and they will find an epitaph for surrealism. A garter snake will crawl up the dress of the shy girl in the corner.

Course Objectives: You will learn that you don't want to be a writer. You will adhere to forms that sound cheap when dead tongues don't speak them. You will learn how to fuck on broken glass. You will learn how to stop dreaming about crimes done by someone else.

Course Topics:
1. Foucault's refutation of artistic madness.
2. The idea of insomnia as a phronesistic imperative.
3. Effective techniques for feeling the grass scream beneath your feet.
4. Why Rimbaud went to Africa, and why you never will.
5. A short history of haiku masters and their rampant bestiality.

Texts and Supplies:
The Digest of Roman Law: Theft, Rapine, Damage, and Insult, by Justinian
Nostalgia for Death and the Hieroglyphs of Desire, by Xavier Villaurrutia

A pair of rusted scissors.
A broken cup.

Grading Plan: You will look into a fogged window on Christmas Eve. Your reflection will rise up slow, and you will say "yes" or "no."

Quizzes: You will repeatedly be required to draw the face of your tormentor and be judged for accuracy and how hard your hand shakes. You will take tranquilizers and write about the trees and the tree things they tell you, and you will expose yourself to them because that's what they want.

Final Exam: The exam will be apprehensive. It will feature fourteen questions. For example, "What about the rose?" "How do you write about a girl with splinters in her eyes?" "Can you hold a can opener until it becomes your friend?"

Attendance: Class is every Sunday at seven in the morning, but you're already here, and early. Un-straighten the chairs until they smile. The lily wasps are sleeping in the drawer. The flag is burning. This used to be a Catholic church, and the altar boys won't leave.

Rules of Conduct: Do not speak when the jackhammers are singing outside the window. Be quiet when the whiteboard writes upon itself in permanent marker. Don't swear because promises are for children who haven't learned to unplug the phone and lock the doors. Don't use attentive language. Cough until a word is stillborn. Slap your face, draw swastikas in drool across your belly, uncomfortably adjust your jeans. Touch yourself until you write something, and then still, until you write well.

Let No Light Enter

no night recede.
We gorge ourselves
on stars and fill
with want.

Close curtain—
freight-heavy
and dark,
the door, lock.

Let the air be
hard perfume,
the weight
of a dead sigh.

I thrum your collarbone
to press notes
onto silence,

to conjure
your crooning,
soft as ghosts.

My face blood-lit,
bent on breaking, never
presses deep
enough to chew
your blooming lungs.

The bed cries too much,
baby with lightning
at her window,

until I spread you out
on the rough carpet—

peel my knees
and flay my hands
in prayer of you.

Tiny soft sunlight.

Love Like Glass Enamel

What I feel laid out
across the brevity of concrete floor.

I show you my broken broom
handle, the sharp bloom of its end
drizzling thin lines across your defiant mouth.

My nauseating breath so heavy,
hard like glass enamel.

I treat you so callous,
so chemical the tears steam
from the dead canyons
of your cheeks.

You wear so well
these blacks and grays,
that tired beneath the eyes'
shade of lavender,

these orphic colors cast
in thick weighted rivers
across the canvas
of your ribs.

I drip virgin white onto your stomach
sunken in from the stench of me.

Your next to nothing tits,
your next to nothing head so tiring.

Two bottles of bourbon coat my bones,
coasting down the highway
with the ghost of Pollock
in a deep black Buick.

In my absence, you suck clean the fur
of brushes, kiss the imprint of my fist
stamped on the door.

You feign, you fool
yourself into desire.

Hands

These hands reach into the sick light of winter,
pulling up the serrated root of a resilient weed
lurking at the corner of a yard, a dying child
burying his fogged silence inside his mother's
sapwood arms.

These weigh the hurt of urns: a stillborn
brother known only as a golden box
with sharpened corners; two
ashed pounds of a father who read Rilke
in prison, pages lit by a sliver of sick light

These hands burn and kill and rest
against the banister—the broken fingers
like eyes peering into the green-glass grin
of an ocean filled with piss, plastics,
and salted choking suicides.

These hands take everything you lend,
a kiss on locked tendons, a chemical whisper,
a match flame building to a soft violet blister:
an erupting question with a tongue of bristled
gray spines.

Dream of the Staircase

I met you at the top of your darkness,
my feet broken through holes in the wood
steps, the railing a rough judgment
like holding the hand of a riot policeman
and moving through a gruesome parade.

The lip of the top step blackened
by your cough, tobacco and bile,
a cancer carnival. I looked in
your milky eye, a white dwarf
cupping the dead, and you said
in a harsh and falling whisper
your dark would become mine

and now I hold it in my skull:
grinding and galled, wriggling,
street-mad, dog-cautious.

If I move a little, so lightly,
eat a perfect egg, flip a pancake,
hum the note of a waking trumpet
just right, the invocation closes
the holes in the stair, the cold railing
grins toothless, and the dark shrinks
down, the thaw of black oak in the Sierra.

I have enough resolve
to take your dark and give it
to the world, spread it out so thin,
so harmless, a splinter in the tender
arch of a child's foot.

Crown of Thorns

Dawn

The center of your eye all-seeing, just
a pomegranate rotted on brown grass—
my want of you the smoke, the smolder,
the nothing of a gutted wood church.

You salted rook who built up lucid pillars
of heavy ash against my blurring eyes:
you labor long and thresh the fleece from earth—
the cold winds at my birth, the blackest blood

tides in my infant brain, you come to bless
arm hooked, slanting hip, thoracic bend:
the mess, the crooked cross of me, the red
words of my hemorrhaging, my first bright death.

A whip you fashion from my breaking spine,
the severed tightrope of my faulted heel.

Mourning

The severed tightrope of my faulted heel
like the blighted dawn cut dead, a hole
in gray paper by hands like feral mouths
that chew through the locked diaries of angels.

There is no light but absent white, a concrete
sheet put down across my leaking eyes.
I soak my soft bound books, my skin in pails
that brim with kerosene—the smell of bacon fat

my bones, and hope a crust of spit now cornered in
my lips, a dried spittoon holds in the bellow
of my bright end: alight the wheat fields, and me
in them: you chaff, you chaff, erased remainder

with your bouquet of brides, voids cut in their eyes,
the screams of children curled in cathode rays.

Meridian

The screams of children curled in cathode rays,
a cold sweat conjured by the alarm clock:
the salt stains on the bed, a lake of black
so like the shadow of the sun pinned in

the sky, a needle through its glowing jaw.
I cannot stand: my bones your last Golgotha.
The feet of angels crush my scalded throat,
their red blades, fake IDs tucked in their robes.

They whisper: don't mind our father, he's done
much worse to us—they drink my whiskey, run
through sprinklers spraying blood, my knees decay

to sand, God's laughter: glass stuck in my hand,
his sunset burns blue like his cloud-bruised girls.

Dusk

His sunset burns blue like his cloud-bruised girls.
or poisoned bowels that burst inside a tramp
who long embraces a torn paper bag—
in sleet and structure fires the bag becomes

the unmistakable shape of his corpse
wife and now another evening corrodes:
the skyline lifeless gray, the wind a groan
of smog and mounting waste, monoxide moans.

The bones of twilight breaking as the bikes
throw laughter down a hill just like a girl
tossed with one shoe from an open trunk:
a radio cries static weeping mothers.

The sidewalks crush the flowers in their seams
and open up with strain to claim their dead.

Nocturne

And open up with strain to claim your dead,
again alight the fields with me in them—
the purple husks of corn my nerves undone,
my muscles bursting like worm-eaten plums.

And break apart my aches, my cricket legs,
the cracked and darkened tablets of my heels:
You smothered your forgiveness in the beds
beneath my jagged nails so I bend

them back like crooked spines until they break,
I suck red sacrament from shouting flesh—
you bleating fish, two handed engine who
threw moon dust into Milton's tea gray eyes.

To cloak the rotting crone you thought was world,
you crafted the bleak body bag of night.

Twilight

You crafted the bleak body bag of night,
and crammed it full of femurs, fawns, and weeds.
It clamors with the hoots of wounded owls—
you throw it down before my splaying feet.

You pluck these blunt edged stars from dark and carve
the cords of me to lepers' melodies—
bones bent and tendons tightly tuned through din.
My guilty judge, you gavel me with pills,

you slash and burn the landscape of my wrists
you grow a desert on my skin, you stitch
my back with locusts for my sins, because
I plucked fruit from her gagging mouth, bit in.

My prayer a feint to thrust the needle through
the center of your eye all-seeing, just.

Little Girl Blue

blind girl choking on sour light
in a deep white basement.

blue girl chewing on a cigarette,
moaning the humid syllables of Mississippi.

dead girl noosed on the door of her closet,
purple faced like a heavy soaked orchid.

black girl burying her tears in dirt,
red dirt, red   as rage.

brown girl washed up from the Rio Grande
tossed from the back of a filthy, gray Cadillac.

sad girl spattered with mosquito kisses,
crying into her mother's aching shoulder.

small girl chewing through her
daddy's hand like a hurt-eyed dog.

Shasta Becomes a Bird

I want to sleep through but one memory:
Mom walking me into the half-lit room,
into the shadow of his gun, the fermenting
silence of her cries, the forest trees a burning
audience to my trembling, my dissolving small hips.

I want to fly from black-gloved whispers.
I want to sleep the dreams of children
who don't know the grunt of a hammer
splintering a mom's head across the driveway.

I'd rather they not tell me God listens.
God watches, another man with a camera
who records what scalds my flat white frame
splayed on the wood, who hangs my brother blue
from a beam like a forgotten Christmas ornament.

When I grow up I'll fit together
blonde strands, severed bracelets,
sobbing palm prints into a picture
of some girl missing like me.

I hold a bludgeoned sunrise
and molten bullets like baby teeth:
my mother's rouged phantom
wipes away my broken moans.

I don't want to see his rusted eyes stain
potassium chloride into gravestone walls.
He strangles my name like a love song,
his voice splitting my small kindling bones.

A Hymn to Your Hip

for Cassady

All the old hens have one, or two if they're lucky,
about their waists like cracked communion plates
as they sit nestled in the nooks
of houses off of Nautilus St.

The dysplastic hum of an offbeat boy who winces,
the shrapnel portrait of a man moving
from the liquor store door, bagged bottle
bullet-lodged under his arm.

Beyond the bone death of my scoliotic every-morning,
the wry motion of your waist awaits, a new nativity cradle
for which my thoughts forsake order, my face drains like a
fished river, and my buttons are loosed.

A scar across your hip the color of a halothane dream,
your hip that holds the shimmer of burnt sidewalks
against my eyes as my nose nestles in your cunt.

Camera Lucida

She twirls like a dish about to shatter,
fallen from her mother's knotted finger—
her sister holds the camera, the frame
trembles like a lamb before a skinner.

She dances, sings this lullaby:
I do this so I can cope with night.

She tears her shirt to strands—
the orange cloth twelve ragged blindfolds
on the floor—and more, her hands

run frightened through the desert of her
belly—salted lines of sweat, those stupid hips,
untreated auburn nest below her naval
forever burnt against that weeping lens.

She opens her lips for the camera,
struggles to name the form within her thighs—
folds like summer, slumber tremors, weeping gore—
her fingers down her throat before, trying to uncoil it.

Her pouted mouth incants this lie:
I do this so I can cope with night.

Down in the Ditch

In the eclipsed afternoon,
my eyes dead tools, my ears plugged
with wet slush, my brain a chipped bell.

This drink is a girl
making snow angels in my stomach,
and all day looks like 6AM

in the timid light,
shadows boasting
as I cross the bridge.

The dampened death

song of the broken stairs—
the deepest syllable beneath my feet.

Down in the ditch
I wait for the train to wail,
grip the grate of the storm drain

and find a loving note,
a lost dog collar,
a rope dropped into the well.

Then the night begins to rain,
a thief who tides away gold dollars,
a black ribbon from a girl's braid.

Soft Violet

I cut the word awake into the small the wave of her shoulder,
but she dare not wade in the salt dead lake of me.
I chew on the red roots of her hair like a dog chews through
belief—

Party dress worn backwards and voice
a rain gutter whispering in pill white winter,
rising white steam from a broken tea cup.

Every morning she folds her body thirty times over
like a careful suicide note and I grow old against that,
curled into the red blood blemish tucked under her left eye.

I spy a skylark asleep on those lips, resting
against the unpronounceable th that slides
from her thoughts of me and thrums
through the shy lines between her teeth.

I want to be a fine needle threaded through
her cheek, a quick shiver cast over the curve
of her ass, a piece of broken glass to salvage—
she licks the blood from her fingers, the blue
of her jeans caught in the January gloom.

That gloom is me, reaching down days
for her name, a soft violet rhyme
with fever dream, blistering, codeine.

Excrement

Sitting loose-boweled in that unnameable coffee shop
thinking about Thomas Aquinas,
my ass carved up like a Christmas bird.

Walking across the dark tar of the hollow
parking lot thinking about the rotting, stinking body:

how excrement seeps brown through blood, a torrent
from the throat mixed with Bombay gin,
a nail bomb bursting in my sour stomach.

Lounging loud-mouthed on the bus, inhaling the scent
of summer blossoms, of gutter bouquets, matted hair,
chewed up gum, the remains of brainless moths.

Standing naked in the hall, bellowing,
"Fuck off and die, Stephen Dedalus."
No matter how strong the denial, I will be glad
to turn the mind off and let the coyotes take the rest.

Driftwood

for Jim Harrison

How does a mouth chew through smoke?
The hinge of the jaw sings out the crunch
of charred branches, the blistered tongue

mutters the red heavy mantra of wildfires
into a black tape recorder, into sun-beaten
granite mistaken for the pulsing throat of a girl.

Our arms outstretched on the mountain ledge,
bodies that fall back against a cross of burnt twigs,
turned to ash and kissed by the tiny beaks of goldfinches.

We fall further down, our mouths
chew the apple skin dusk on the wordless bank
of a river, its murmurs stitched mute with dark moss and clay.

We craft poles from driftwood and failure,
cast one milky eye on the dusty green water,
filled with wolves' thirst for the marrow of words.

Alexandria

I sit beside you in the budding dark, a penitent
fallen through the confessional wall—tomorrow
you wake early for mass, with these crude jokes
and my long glances tucked into the small white
pocket of a blouse your mother pressed neat.

In nineteen years alive the only thing I know
sacred and burning is this want, you small bunting
smothered in brandy: a dream where you unfold
the newly soiled red napkin pressed in your sex
and place it prayer heavy on my tongue.

The small embers of dust coughed from the couch
carve a path through the broken lamp that shudders
light over the lost marble of your nose, your close
trimmed hair like Joan of Arc, ocean eyed and lips
kissed to the sand blasted cheek of a faceless god.

You reach your hand across the sea of a broken
cushion and I look through the hole in your palm, the buttons
on your cotton shirt sealed like a covenant, the sea
of your mouth parted but an inch, the wave
of its small whimper I crash against, resist.

I carve a path back to my room alone, thankful
to know you'll forget me like the fragment
of a psalm crushed in the dirt, or the litany
I whispered in reverse against your earlobe
as my hand stopped cold above your giving knees.

You Will Be Gray

The creak of the deadbolt,
the break of the gravel beneath
my step will be your welcoming.

Like the gravel, the cracks
in the road, the rubbish bins—

you will be gray.

You will be the last cloud
covering my springtime,
I will talk to you about honors
and awards, a quiet porch
covered in cigar smoke
and the sighs of an old dog,
a warm love by the table
in morning,
and you will say no.

You will stand in my driveway,
the break of the gravel beneath
your step as the trash bag falls
from my hand sounding sick
like a child's broken wrist,
like a fall from a bicycle
into a pool of frozen lights.

You will have waited long enough.

Douglas Payne studied Poetry in the MFA program at Arizona State University. His writing has appeared in *The Far East: Everything Just as It Is, Shot Glass Journal*, the daily blog of author Dennis Cooper, and elsewhere..

www.ingramcontent.com/pod-product-compliance
Lightning Source LLC
Chambersburg PA
CBHW021454080526
44588CB00009B/840